TIME IN EDUCATION: INTERTWINED DIMENSIONS AND THEORETICAL POSSIBILITIES

TIME IN EDUCATION
INTERTWINED DIMENSIONS AND THEORETICAL POSSIBILITIES

CATHERINE COMPTON-LILLY

GARN PRESS WOMEN SCHOLARS SERIES

BOBBIE KABUTO
SENIOR EDITOR

GARN PRESS
NEW YORK, NY

Published by Garn Press, LLC
New York, NY
www.garnpress.com

Copyright © 2020 by Catherine Compton-Lilly and Bobbie Kabuto (editor), except as noted below

Garn Press and the Chapwoman logo are registered trademarks of Garn Press: LLC. All rights reserved. No part of this publication may be reproduced, distributed, or transmitted in any form or by any means, including photocopying, recording, or other electronic or mechanical methods, without the prior written permission of the publisher, except in the case of brief quotations embodied in critical reviews and certain other noncommercial uses permitted by copyright law. For permission requests, please contact Garn Press through *www.garnpress.com*.

The chapter of this book titled *Time In Education: Intertwined Dimensions and Theoretical Possibilities* by Catherine Compton-Lilly is © 2015. It was first published online on June 15, 2015, and subsequently in the November 1, 2016 issue of the Sage journal *Time & Society*, Volume 25, Issue 3, pages 575-593, and is reprinted here by permission

Book and cover design by Ben James Taylor

Library of Congress Control Number: 2020936759

Publisher's Cataloging-in-Publication Data

Names: Compton-Lilly, Catherine | Kabuto, Bobbie.
Title: Time in Education: Intertwined Dimensions and Theoretical Possibilities / Catherine Compton-Lilly and Bobbie Kabuto (editor).
Description: Description: New York: Garn Press, 2020. | Includes bibliographical references.
Identifiers: LCCN 2020936759 | ISBN 978-1-942146-80-3 (pbk.) | 978-1-942146-79-7 (Kindle ebook).
Subjects: LCSH: Education--Research. | Literacy. | Critical theory. | Critical pedagogy. | Language arts. | BISAC: EDUCATION / Urban. | EDUCATION / Multicultural Education. | EDUCATION / Curricula. | EDUCATION / Parent Participation. | EDUCATION / Research.
Classification: LCC LB1050.9.c23 2020 (print) |LCC LB1050.9 (ebook) | DDC 370.028--dc23.
Library of Congress record available at https://lccn.loc.gov/2020936759.

TABLE OF CONTENTS

Editor's Introduction: Bobbie Kabuto	1
Families and Schooling	3
Time in Educational Research	10
A Year in Time	12
Researching Time	21
References	24
Time in Education: Intertwined Dimensions and Theoretical Possibilities: Catherine Compton-Lilly	27
My Trajectory as a Researcher	31
Introducing Marvin	37
Temporal Dimensions of Three Theories	38
Lemke's Timescales	39
The Library as an Icon of Possibility	41
Bakhtin's Chronotope	45
The Construction of Failure	49
Bourdieu's Habitus	54
Possibilities of Being and Becoming	57

What do Theoretical Understandings about Time Offer Educators?	63
References	75

An Interview with Catherine Compton-Lilly: Bobbie Kabuto	82
List of Selected Works by Catherine Compton-Lilly	90
Catherine Compton-Lilly: A Short Biography	94
Bobbie Kabuto: A Short Biography	96
Garn Press Women Scholars Series	99
Negotiating a Permeable Curriculum: On Literacy, Diversity, and the Interplay of Children's and Teachers' Worlds	99
Teaching without Testing: Assessing the Complexity of Children's Literacy Learning	100
Time in Education: Intertwined Dimensions and Theoretical Possibilities	101
Great Women Scholars: Yetta Goodman, Maxine Greene, Louise Rosenblatt, Margaret Meek Spencer	103

EDITOR'S INTRODUCTION
BOBBIE KABUTO

From the first day of kindergarten to the day that their children graduate high school, families organize their lives around school-based timeframes down to the year, month, day, and even minute. Children have to be in school by a certain time, and sometimes families have to struggle around work schedules to make sure their children are cared for before and after school. Some families have a time for starting homework, and others plan vacations around the school calendar. Families whose children are in school live within chronological timelines organized by different types of calendars like the Roman calendar or the Lunar calendar, while simultaneously living within school-based timelines, such as the change in a grade or a school year.

Despite the complex cartography of time that consolidates, arranges, structures, and categories the experiences of families, educational structures attempt to provide a uniform way of systemizing concepts like *development*, *ability*, and *learning* around reading and writing. Benchmarking and content standards, such as those represented by the Common Core State Standards, are broken down to grade levels so that by the end of each grade level students are expected to meet a benchmark or standard for performing at grade level expectations.

Within educational systems, psychological processes are assumed to be measured within a socially constructed system of time such as grade level, that may have little to do with other timeframes, such as biological, physical, or historical. As Sorokin (1943) would argue, time organized within school-based frames – such as grade level, vacation breaks, and changes in school years – has a social and cultural nature that gives a rhythm to our social lives.

This edition of the Women Scholars Series will further explore the intersection of literacy and the construct of time within education through the work of Catherine Compton-Lilly. Originally published in *Time and Society, Time in Education: Intertwined Dimensions and Theoretical Possibilities* highlights the complexity of studying the concept of *learning* and how and what people learn over time within school-based structures. These structures were designed to not only organize educational experiences, but they also have built in power structures that define who we are as learners, privileging certain type of learners and marginalizing others (Ball, 2016).

At the same time, Compton-Lilly presents a theoretical kaleidoscope of studying learning and literacy over time, and she illustrates how our perspective of a learner can change as we rotate different theoretical lenses. The question that arises is how do we reconcile, or do we need to reconcile, these sometimes complementary or contradictory framings of learners? This is a dilemma that I have faced within my own research in working with families to better understand how and why parents support or challenge school-based definitions of their children as learners.

FAMILIES AND SCHOOLING

In 2003, Compton-Lilly introduced the educational community to her first book, *Reading Families: The Literate Lives of Urban Children*. Through the study of discourse, Compton-Lilly expanded the field of family literacy and the works of Heath (1983), Taylor (1983), and Taylor and Dorsey-Gaines (1988). *Reading Families* is based on Compton-Lilly's experiences as a first-grade teacher that led her to study families in urban settings. In this current volume, Compton-Lilly reflected on her past research for *Reading Families*:

> While the neighborhood around my school struggled economically and media reports about the community focused on drugs arrests and shootings, I continued to be impressed by the resilience and commitment to children exhibited by family members despite the lack of resources.

As a teacher-researcher, Compton-Lilly interviewed, visited the homes of, and collected school documents for ten of her first grade African American students. The culmination of this work illustrated not only the literacy practices of nine students, it also inserted issues of equity and marginalization into researching and studying families of color.

The field of family literacy has highlighted the mismatches between home and school. The grounding break ethnographic work of Heath (1983) provided deep insights into the border conflicts at the mismatch of home and school literacy practices. This research lead other researchers to consider how "success" and "failure" had more to do with mirroring school-based practices and ideologies than it did with any sanitized notion of educational ability.

Taylor and Dorsey-Gaines (1988) were among the first researchers to study families living in urban, inner-city areas. They effectively illustrated the diverse literate practices of the inner-city families and how they supported their children's educational experiences as they navigated home and school literacy practices. In spite of their abilities, Taylor and Dorsey Gaines (1988) argued for the children, "Their daily lives and their complex social and cognitive communicative abilities were not relevant to the definitions of school learning, which were limited by the exercises that were given and the tests that were set" (p. 209).

Like Taylor and Dorsey-Gaines, Compton-Lilly put issues of identity, race, poverty, agency, and power at the heart of her discussion in *Reading Families*. In describing the purpose of the book, Compton-Lilly (2003) wrote:

> This book explores how generally accepted discourses concerning the use of literacy and the possibilities created through literacy learning operate within a community in which many families have been denied access to mainstream ways of life that many people take for granted (safe communities, homes that meet safety codes, jobs that provide a living way, health diets, adequate educational experiences). Pages 5-6.

Compton-Lilly (2003) suggested that families living in urban communities were stereotypically portrayed as being at odds with schooling. She explained:

> In contrast to the stereotypes of urban parents that portray them as unconcerned about their children's academic progress, the parents I interviewed taught me otherwise. Parents consistently expressed their strong beliefs about the importance of reading in their children's lives, and no parent ever questioned the value and importance of reading; parents felt that reading was among the things children needed for "survival." Pages 4-5.

Compton-Lilly's findings uncovered many assumptions around urban families. She argued that assumptions such as "urban families of color are lacking in education and resources" or "are uninterested in schooling," were:

> ... generally based on media depictions and an urban mythology that attempts to explain the academic difficulties of urban schools by blaming parents or offering simplistic notions of teacher incompetence (poor pedagogy, lazy and uncaring teachers). Page 10.

Compton-Lilly (2007b) further explained how children's actual abilities in school can be overshadowed by other types of capital forms, such as behavior, the ability to speak English, and economics.

Four years after her initial study, Compton-Lilly returned to the families to provide a longitudinal examination, presented in the book *Re-Reading Families: The Literate Lives of Urban Children, Four Years Later* (Compton-Lilly, 2007a). As a sequel to *Reading Families*, *Re-Reading Families* presented a "re-reading of the children and their families" in order to "revisit and re-examine their literacy learning over time" (Compton-Lilly, 2015, page 62). It was within this context that Compton-Lilly took an interest in time and temporality. As Compton-Lilly wrote in *Re-Reading Families*:

> Time haunts me as a researcher. I contemplate the trajectories that awaited my former students and the severe consequences of attending underfunded schools in a high poverty community. I recall my amazing six-year-old students and the potential they brought to my classroom. I consider the parents' unwavering hope for their children's futures. I lament the opportunities they did not find in school, the stifling instruction that they reported, and the failed tests, low report card grades, and stringent behavioral policies that they recalled.

Five years after *Re-Reading Families* was published, Compton-Lilly again returned to the same families. In her book, *Reading Time: The Literate Lives of Urban Secondary Students and*

Their Families (Compton-Lilly, 2012), she revisited the children as middle school students. While the research continued to focus on literacy, the accounts of students and their parents extended to school policies and practices as well as peers and popular culture. As she spoke with students and their parents, again, time proved to be salient. She explained:

> Students and parents revisited experiences from their past, compared the past to the present, spoke of the pace of instruction, described progress in school, and their hopes for the future. Based on these accounts, I argue that humans are temporal beings, and time plays a significant role in literacy learning, identity construction, and schooling. Page 1.

In 2017, Compton-Lilly published the final book in this series, *Reading Students' Lives: Literacy Learning Across Time*, which followed the children into high school. While spaces of hope and possibility continued to be evident across the cases, it was clear that the challenges that accompanied attending an underfunded school in an underfunded community had taken its toll on the students and their families. Some students were retained in school multiple times, while others experienced altercations with the law. Most left school. Some continued to aspire towards college.

Compton-Lilly turned her attention to equity,

arguing that "this longitudinal study contributes to understandings about how the achievement debt continues to operate in innocuous and devastating ways across time" (page 119). She highlighted the importance of research that attends to temporality, arguing that:

> ... longitudinal conversations must recognize the long-term trajectories of *becoming* as students move through school. People's social histories, both individually lived and historically imposed matter and these histories continuously converge in the lives of individuals. Page 121.

Thus, revisiting these families revealed the confluence of students' trajectories, families' histories, and larger social histories that defined both schools and American society – including the inequities that continue to operate.

Referencing the concept of revisiting, Sefton-Green (2015) suggested that returning to previous research sites and participants allows researchers to study how participants contend with changes in their experiences over time, or how they 're-experience,' particularly as they attempt to reconcile past and present experiences to see future trajectories and goals.

In my own research, I discuss this mobilization of meaning through re-experiencing over time as transgenerational within families. Within a transgenerational perspective of family literacy, I reconsider how *family* does not necessarily mean the immediate family at any given time. Rather, a transgenerational perspective forefronts the historicity of the family and understanding how past experiences relate to decisions in the present.

For instance, parents may draw upon their own educational histories to make sense of, not just experiences on longer timescales like their children's performance from grade to grade, but also of situated experiences on shorter time scales, like reading a sentence. Consequently, families carry and construct models and beliefs about learning that are solidified through activities and relationships that families have with other people and institutions such as schools.

These models and beliefs emerge out the stories that families tell, and as Compton-Lilly (2011) argued, parents "repeatedly returned to some stories while neglecting and forgetting others or framed some stories as examples of larger patterns" (page 248).

TIME IN EDUCATIONAL RESEARCH

In this Women's Scholar Series, Compton-Lilly explores the concept of *time as context* to challenge learning as static or linearly progressive. In an enlightening discussion of the plurality of time across the social and physical sciences,

Sorokin (1943) outlines different conceptions of time. More importantly, Sorokin effectively illustrates how these different conceptions of time can be confused and conflated within sociocultural contexts, particularly in the discourses that individuals employ to make sense of their lived experiences.

Some of the conceptualization of time include physicomathematical time, biological time and psychological time, all of which have been of interest to the fields of education. For instance, researchers in early writing have painstakingly documented the development of writing through inventive spellings (Kamii & Manning, 2002; Masterson & Apel, 2010) and name writing (Both-de Vries & Bus, 2008). Other researchers have documented the development of writing and drawing forms and name writing (Clay, 1975; Puranik & Lonigan, 2011). This body of research has led to the idea of predictability and orderable stages in writing development. When children do not progress across stages in an anticipated fashion, then families or teachers become concerned and talk about children as "working below age- and grade- level expectations". These discussions can cause families to search out educational professionals for testing and evaluation.

What is talked little about is how, as researchers and educators, we have used these time concepts to construct ideas and beliefs around learners' abilities. As Sorokin (1943) argued, "Observation shows that persons equally old according to the physical clock are physiologically at quite different stages of development" (p. 163). Yet there are areas in educational research that attempt to normalize development, create age- and grade- level expectations, and require students to make adequate yearly progress. We treat words like *age*, *grade*, and *year* as static, neutral numbers that measure consistent and continuous phenomena when they are, in fact, words with socially constructed and evolving meanings. To provide an illustration of how families use discourses around time to talk about, frame, and make sense of their children as readers and literate individuals, I will describe how the concept of *year* indexed a variety of meanings within families' lived experiences, was defined through sociocultural meanings, and acted a discourse connector and time-bridge to the past as families constructed their understandings of the present.

A YEAR IN TIME

In the study *Revaluing Readers and Families* (Kabuto, 2015), I have examined the ways in which school-based structures intersect and reconstruct family structures. Studying seven families, I had a particular interest in how families understood themselves in relation to a myriad of school-based concepts such as "learning disabled," "language disorder," "Attention Deficit Disorder," and "dual-language learner." Through the 90 hours of audiotaped data, which included interviews and parents and their children orally reading and reflecting with each other, the families in the study exemplified how they understood their experiences around school-based concepts through the *context of time* (Compton-Lilly, this volume). In other words, school-based timeframes not only synchronized familial routines, they also provided a point of reference in or entry into understanding and discussing their children's learning and progress in school. These points of reference epitomize the time-bending nature of discourse, or how discourse is a means to "recursively revisit some experiences" and make sense of "the tensions that accompany school trajectories, and the long-term embodiment of ways of being – including ways of being literate" (Compton-Lilly, this volume).

Within the 90 hours of audiotaped discourse, the families used the concept of year to organize their experiences around schooling. Consider the following examples from the parents when they discussed their children's progress in school:

> **Terry:** I wish you could meet her [my daughter's] classroom teacher. They saw a little something going on. They were going to test her [and] we said we're not

waiting until next **year**. We're going to go ahead and test her. It's not likely [but] it's a possibility [because] the other two have trouble.

Donna: This is the last **year's** book and it wasn't hard enough so I asked the teacher for the activities.

Nancy: For a **year** and a half, I kept asking what they [the teachers] are doing and they could never tell me what they were doing.

Maria: Which ever book is more exciting she will like better. I don't like Jenny's teacher because she is not as attentive as her teacher from last **year**. Hopefully next **year** she'll have a better teacher.

Francis: This **year** it has so far has been challenging. I have been less strict this **year** and her grades have dropped. This has been very strange for me.

Carole: She works with a special ed [education] teacher who throws them all together and throws Wilson [Reading Program] at them because that's what comes up for reading purposes based on the initial evaluation. So it's nothing. At least, though, she's been a very good girl and participating in the group reading in the classroom last **year** and the beginning of this **year.**

In each of these examples, the mothers use the term *year* to measure a grade-level rather than a calendar year, and using the concept of year as a school-based structure allowed the mothers to index some point in time in their children's experiences in school. These points in time may have described a performance measure, such as in Francis' comment. Being concerned about her daughter Sophie's progress in the fourth grade, Francis further explained her concerns by stating, "This **year** Sophie brings home 70's and 60's while last **year** she brought home A's."

The process of classification and declassification were also events that the mothers tracked throughout grade-level constructs. This point is exemplified in Terry's comment about her youngest daughter's progress in school. Her two older children were classified in school from the first grade. Because her youngest daughter was in kindergarten, she felt that she should wait until the first grade to start the process for classification.

Year as a school-based structure also referenced programs and curricular materials for the families. Donna's, Nancy's, and Carole's comments illustrate this point. Donna expressed frustration that the school did not academically challenge her daughter, who was diagnosed with a pervasive developmental disorder not otherwise specified (PDD-NOS), as well as a speech and language impairment. She often approached the teachers to ask for work that she could take home to do with Nina. Donna's comment above refers to an unchallenging book that Nina, who was in the fourth grade, read when she was in the third grade.

Nancy expressed a similar frustration. Since Becky was in the first grade when she was classified with a learning disability, Nancy often inquired about the types of reading instruction that the teachers provided Becky, or asked about strategies that she could use with Becky at home. Nancy expressed frustrations about the Committee for Special Education (CSE) meetings and the lack of concern they exhibited to her comments and questions. Similarly, Carole, with dismay, discussed how the school used the Wilson Program for her daughter. While Carole could not attest to the effectiveness of the program, she noted that Christie had participated in the program beginning in the second grade.

Mothers spoke about their daughters' experiences in terms of years. The concept of "year," however, held sociocultural meanings and social references to time, rather than representing a continuous, measureable, and mechanical span of time. How the mothers' used discourses related to time were coordinated by the school-based culture and milieu within which these families lived. Furthermore, the concept of year as a school-based structure illustrates how time is an extension of memory and synchronization of past and present activities – or provides a context to make sense of the experiences of their children's successes and struggles in school, as illustrated in the discourses above.

Carole and her daughter Christie's case study provide a powerful example of the contextual nature of time. Out of the seven families, I followed two of them over time, engaging in the process of revisiting as described earlier in this introduction. I first met the family when Christie was in kindergarten. They began participation in the study when Christie was in first grade (Phase 1), and I revisited them when Christie was in third grade (Phase 2). My last revisit was when Christie was in the eleventh grade (Phase 3). Christie was classified with a speech and language disability when she entered kindergarten. I have written extensively about various parts of my research with Carole and Christie, and I have now begun to look across my research encounters with them to understand how Christie has understood herself as a literate individual working within the special education system.

To examine how time provides a context to understanding one's experiences, I examined how Carole and Christie used the concept of year in relation to past, present, and future experiences. There were two notable findings I gleaned from the data. First, the term *year* increased per session over each phase of the study. For instance, the concept of year appeared three times in session 1 of the first-grade data (one example was presented above), nine times in the session 1 of the third-grade data, and sixteen times in session 1 of the eleventh-grade data. Furthermore, when the concept of a year occurred in each of the phases of the study, it indexed events on a longer timescale.

For instance, over the phases of the study, Carole regularly returned to her frustration at the type of reading instruction that Christie received in school. As noted above, Carole described how Christie participated in the Wilson Program. When Christie was in third grade, Carole advocated for Christie to work with a reading specialist. Carole described, "I met her [the reading specialist] at the evaluation. They finally gave it to us after all this asking… at the end of the **year**. It'll be the last six weeks of school." Not only did Carole use the concept of a year as a school-based structure to discuss the services her daughter had received, she also used the concept as a way to monitor her daughter's growth and maturity as a reader. During our first session in Phase 2 of the study, Christie read *Little Blue and Little Yellow* (Lionni, 1969), and Carole asked about the difficulty level of the book. In order to make sense of Christie's oral reading performance, she compared it to how she thought Christie had read the previous year. Carole said, "You did awesome. You know a **year** ago you would not have been able to read the story with her [Christie]. There's a certain maturity about her that she did not have one **year** ago."

As these examples illustrate, Carole used the concept of a year as a school-based structure to contextualize and make sense of what she was observing. This theme occurred across data from the seven families. When the families used a year as a school-based structure, they used the term as a time-bridge to connect past experiences with present ones. This was particularly true in the case of Christie as she attempted to make sense of her mounting experiences in special education that would eventually cause her to graduate high school at 19 or 20 years of age.

Christie was more vocal when I revisited her in eleventh-grade, and her use of "year" began to extend over longer timeframes. Christie explained:

> Yeah. And I'm bad in math now – it's like I'm in Algebra. But math will take me a while to practice, because I've been in basic math and also the life skills. So that's going to be 10 times worse, because middle school destroyed me. Like the whole **year** in middle school, because I have to be in life skills.

In this example, Christie explained how math had become a difficult subject for her by returning to her experiences in middle school, when the CSE tried to place her on the life skills path which incorporated 'basic math.' Christie's use of year connected back to her middle school experiences as she explained not only how she was resistant to being placed on a life-skills path in school, but also how she started attending her CSE meetings in order to vocalize her objections. Christie felt that being placed in life skills had had a negative impact on her learning, and that being in basic math had held her back from being successful in math in eleventh-grade. Consequently, the word "year" was not a mathematical connector in time, rather it was a sociocultural connector so that her past experiences assisted her in making sense of more current ones. Similar to Marvin (Compton-Lilly, this volume), Christie had to negotiate "a school system filled with expectations and tracked instructional experiences". As Compton-Lilly further explained, "The instructional experiences he [Marvin] experienced – heavy-handed discipline, low expectations, special education placement, retention, and racism – informed his sense of self and the dispositions that he brought forward."

These discourse samples illustrate how making sense of and interpreting one's learning experiences are as much about as one's historicity as they are about experiencing events in the present. Occurrences in the present are not decontextualized activities, instead they often reflect a re-experiencing of connected or related activities. Each time activities are re-experienced, they are given new and renewed meanings.

RESEARCHING TIME

In the next section of this book, Compton-Lilly provides an in-depth perspective of "time as context" by presenting three different and interrelated perspectives for framing time in educational research. After re-introducing Marvin from *Reading Families*, Compton-Lilly takes the reader through a kaleidoscope that repositions Marvin's experience in school, which "was often punctuated by altercations with other students and run-ins with teachers". With each slight turn in the kaleidoscope, readers have the opportunity to grasp how, as Compton-Lilly explains, time is "a significant contextual dimension that contributes to how people make sense of themselves, their experiences, and their worlds."

Building on the work of Bakhtin's (1981, 1986) concept of chronotopes, other researchers have argued for a more integrated discussion of time in educational research. For instance, Boylan (n.d.) proposed the idea of expansiveness in mathematics education based on expansive chronotopes. Boylan contrasts expansive chronotopes with regulated time in education, which mirrors an industrial timescale that "denies the historicity of the learner" as "the orientation is on the future and on outcomes" (p. 16). White and Pham (2017) further suggest how chronotopes can be used as a tool to understand how students author themselves as English language learners, and how to include discussions of agency and emotion into the idea of timescapes.

It is here that I invite readers into realms of time to consider how discourses around time, the ways that we use time to organize our lives, and how time as context are used for making sense of our students' experiences. As Sorokin (1943) wrote:

> We have broken man's life into mathematically equal units of time and computed its duration in these units, as a result, man's life has slipped between our fingers. The meaningfulness, the essential states through which it passes, all the characteristics of these stages – in brief, almost the whole content of man's life – disappeared in our numbers. P. 203

Students like Marvin and Christie are more than numbers that describe individuals who are incarcerated, graduate high school after four years, or are in special education. Compton-Lilly's work in this Women Scholars Series presents a powerful example of how "all [that] is left is a row of numbers, like millions of other rows indicating the mean, the median, the mode" when meaning is removed from those numbers (Sorokin, 1943, 203).

REFERENCES

Ball, S. (2016). *Foucault, power, and education.* New York, NY: Routledge.

Both-de Vries, A. C., & Bus, A. G. (2008). Name writing: A first step to phonetic writing? Does the name have a special role in understanding the symbolic function of writing? *Literacy, Teaching and Learning, 12*(2), 37.

Boylan, M. (n.d). Towards a mathematics education for ecological selves: Pedagogies for relational knowing and being. Retrieved from: http://socialsciences.exeter.ac.uk/education/research/centres/stem/publications/pmej/pome32/Boylan-submitted.docx

Clay, M. (1975). *What did I write?: Beginning writing behavior.* Portsmouth, NH: Heinemann.

Compton-Lilly, C. (2003). *Reading families: The literate lives of urban children.* New York, NY: Teachers College Press.

Compton-Lilly, C. (2007a). *Re-reading families: The literate lives of urban children, four years later.* New York, NY: Teachers College Press.

Compton-Lilly, C. (2007b). The complexities of reading in two Puerto Rican families. *Reading Research Quarterly, 42*(1), 72-98.

Compton-Lilly, C. (2011). Literacy and schooling in one family across time. *Research in the Teaching of English, 45*(3), 224-251.

Compton-Lilly, C. (2015). Revisiting children and families: Temporal discourse analysis and the longitudinal construction of meaning. In J. Sefton-Green & J. Rowsell (Eds.), *Learning and literacy over time: Longitudinal perspectives* (pp. 61-78). New York, NY: Routledge.

Heath, S. B. (1983). *Ways with words: Language, life, and work in communities and classrooms.* New York, NY: Cambridge.

Kabuto, B. (2015). Transgenerational learning within families. *Journal of Family Diversity in Education, 1*(4), 45-65

Kamii, C., & Manning, M. (2002). Phonemic awareness and beginning reading and writing. *Journal of Research in Childhood Education, 17*(1), 38-46.

Lionni, L. (1959). *Little blue and little yellow.* New York, NY: Harper Collins.

Masterson, J. J., & Apel, K. (2010). The Spelling Sensitivity Score: Noting developmental changes in spelling knowledge. *Assessment for Effective Intervention, 36*(1), 35-45.

Puranik, C. S., & Lonigan, C. J. (2011). From scribbles to scrabble: Preschool children's developing knowledge of written language.

Reading and Writing, 24(5), 567-589.

Sefton-Green, J. (2015). Introduction: Making sense of longitudinal perspectives on literacy learning – A revisiting approach. In J. Sefton-Green & J. Rowsell (Eds.), *Learning and literacy over time: Longitudinal perspectives* (pp. 1-15). New York: Routledge.

Sorokin, P. (1943). *Sociocultural causality, space, time: A student of referential principles of sociology and social science.* Durham, NC: Duke University Press.

Taylor, D. (1983). *Family literacy: Young children learning to read and write.* Portsmouth: Heinemann.

Taylor, D., & Dorsey-Gaines, C. (1988). *Growing up literate: Learning from inner-city families.* Portsmouth, NH: Heinemann.

White, C., & Pham, C. (2017). Time in the experience of agency and emotion in English language learning in rural Vietnam. *Innovation in Language Learning and Teaching, 11*(3), 207-218.

TIME IN EDUCATION: INTERTWINED DIMENSIONS AND THEORETICAL POSSIBILITIES

CATHERINE COMPTON-LILLY

Giddens (1991) argued that few things in life as are commonplace as time. Time constantly passes as people allocate hours of their days and organize their lives. However, time is generally treated as a backdrop to experience and rarely contemplated as a significant contextual dimension that contributes to how people make sense of themselves, their experiences, and their worlds. For the past several years, I have explored time as a constitutive dimension of people's experiences that significantly affects how people make sense of themselves and their worlds.

Recognizing *time as context* is paramount to understanding how children and families make sense of literacy and school experiences. However, literacy researchers have generally failed to recognize the temporal nature of people's experiences and the longitudinal construction of meaning. This neglect of time can be traced to methodologies that generally involve relatively short-term snapshots of children's lives – 6 months, 1 year, and 3 years.

Because little qualitative research tracks children, teachers, or literacy development over long periods of time the full impact of long-term situations – living in high poverty communities, attending poorly funded schools, and being subjected to often oppressive instruction – has not been recognized. Researchers generally fail to recognize and appreciate the ways in which students selectively and recursively revisit some experiences, the tensions that accompany school trajectories, and the long-term embodiment of ways of being – including ways of being literate.

In this examination of time in schooling, I explore time in my own trajectory as a literacy scholar. I consider my own journey as a researcher following students over time alongside my transition from being a first-grade teacher to being a university scholar. Next, I present empirical data from a ten-year longitudinal study to explore the affordances of temporal analyses in educational research. My goal is not to explore findings from the study; these are explored elsewhere (Compton-Lilly, 2003, 2007, 2012, 2016). My goal is to examine the affordances of three theoretical perspectives for enabling literacy researchers to attend to how students construct meaning over time as they move through school.

Drawing on scholarship that presents time as multidimensional and intersectional (Adam, 1989, 2000; Schatzki, 2006), I challenge the notion of time as a simple, singular, and linear contextual dimension of people's experiences. Instead, I explore time as entailing multiple and overlapping dimensions that significantly affect how people make sense of themselves and their worlds. Adam (1989, 2000) situates time and space within "timescapes" (2000, p. 125) in which phenomena are encountered, processes are enacted, and events are experienced. She challenges social science researchers to maintain the complexity of situations and experiences that complicate time as simply passing. As Adam notes, "A focus on time highlights multiple realities that all bear on social life simultaneously" (Adam, 1989, p. 458).

The construct of timescape acknowledges the "spatial and temporal features of a social situation as well as the importance of the wider context. Moreover, time is conceived as not one but multidimensional" (Adam, 2003b, p. 96). Many scholars have recognized the multidimensional nature of time (Bidart, 2012; Cipriani, 2013; Firth & Robinson, 2014; Keightley, 2013). For example, Facer, Joiner, Stanton, Reid, Hull, and Kirk (2004) explore how technology can be used to provide opportunities for students to physically enact and interact within scenarios that support embodied activity within time – moving, thinking, talking, acting, planning, and ultimately learning.

To explore the multidimensional nature of time, I present my own trajectory. I then apply the work of three highly influential theorists – Lemke (2000), Bakhtin (1981, 1986), and Bourdieu (1980/1990, 1991) – to examine various temporal dimensions of schooling and learning as experienced by Marvin, one of my former students who participated in my ten-year longitudinal study. Each theory reveals critical insights into the roles time plays in educational spaces. Specifically, I argue that Lemke's notion of timescales highlights the temporally layered experiences that people draw upon to make sense of their worlds (Lemke, 2000). Bakhtin's description of chronotope invites the exploration of cumulating motifs and tropes that accompany being a successful or unsuccessful student (Bakhtin, 1986).

Finally, Bourdieu's notion of habitus draws our attention to the embodied ways of being that children assume early in life and carry with them across time (Bourdieu, 1971, 1980/1990; Bourdieu & Passeron, 1977). While I do not begin to claim that any one of these theories presents a comprehensive understanding of time, I propose that each theory contributes to thinking about the multidimensional nature of time and complicates time as a significant dimension of experience. Prior to presenting Marvin's story, I first present my own longitudinal becoming.

MY TRAJECTORY AS A RESEARCHER

In 1996, I was a first-grade teacher and doctoral student. I had worked in the same school for the prior eight years. While the neighborhood around my school struggled economically and media reports about the community focused on drugs arrests and shootings, I continued to be impressed by the resilience and commitment to children exhibited by family members despite the lack of resources. Larger issues related to social justice operated in this community. At the time of my study, there was no grocery store within ten miles of my school despite it being located in the middle of a city. The local library was in the process of being closed and the children were not allowed to play on the school playground due to disrepair and safety issues.

I taught at Rosa Parks Elementary School, a large urban school where 97% of the students qualified for free or reduced-price lunch. The children and their families lived in the housing projects and apartments that surrounded my school. While the neighborhood was characterized as violent and drug infested by the local media, I was continually impressed by the dedicated and compassionate parents who brought or sent their children to our school each day. My school was an underfunded elementary school located in this high poverty community, and one of the first schools in the country to be placed on our State's list of failing schools. Marvin was one of the children in my first-grade classroom.

For my doctoral dissertation, I conducted a teacher research study that explored the literacy practices of ten of my African American and Puerto Rican students. To begin my doctoral dissertation and document the literacy practices of my students and their families, I contacted the parents in alphabetical order as I moved down my class list. They all agreed to participate. Eventually, the families participated in the study when my former students were in grades one, five, eight, and eleven. During grade one, I collected multiple classroom observations and student work samples. During each phase of the project, I interviewed children and parents. When the children were in high school, I was awarded a grant from the Spencer Foundation that enabled me to visit children at school and interview their teachers. The year I collected the data for my dissertation, we faced the threat of being closed by the State unless our reading and math test scores improved.

During each phase of the longitudinal study, I collected reading assessments (Ekwall & Shanker, 1993, Leslie & Caldwell, 2006) and writing samples. Throughout the study, children and parents were asked about their reading practices, their use of technology, and their satisfaction with school. Children and parents described their favorite books and their plans for the future. Over time, children and families increasingly discussed school expectations and the challenges they faced at school. Thus, the focus of the study expanded beyond literacy as identity negotiations, school policies, and peer relationships became increasingly salient.

Across the study, data analysis involved transcription followed by a grounded coding of interviews and field notes (Strauss & Corbin, 1990). I soon learned that longitudinal analysis is inherently temporal. At times, data collected during an early phase of the research gained significance when viewed in relation to data collected years later. These longitudinal patterns were not well served by my separate attempts to code data from each phase of the project.

Longitudinal analysis required an additional time-consuming process of reading, and rereading stacks of data as well as using the search function on my word processor as particular words and ideas reemerged across the data set. While my teacher research perspective and my field notes were informed by my proximity to the children and our shared experiences in the classroom, my researcher perspective benefited from the luxury of revisiting data across a decade and by the application of multiple analytic procedures and theoretical frames.

I am now an endowed professor at the University of South Carolina, Columbia. Obtaining tenure at a top-ranked university involved a complicated dance. I needed to establish a presence in the literacy world, publish in the "best" journals, adhere to established writing norms, and cite the right scholars. The Internal Review Board process, my relationships with senior scholars, and the politics of professional organizations influence what I study. I have avowedly enjoyed benefits from this transition from teacher to scholar. In short, I have retired from the demanding life of a classroom teacher allowing me the privilege of thinking and writing about students that I taught two decades ago.

Meanwhile, time has also passed for my former students and their families. When I was a teacher, I was in my late 30's. The children's parents were approximately my age. Since then many of us have become grandparents and some of my former students have children of their own. Some parents have retired and more than one parent has passed away.

Eventually, my dissertation became a book

and I assumed a position at the University of Wisconsin, Madison. My research with my former students did not end with my move to the university. Instead, I stayed in touch with my former first grade students and their families as the students moved through high school. I have written extensively about these students over the past 20 years.

Time haunts me as a researcher. I contemplate the trajectories that awaited my former students and the severe consequences of attending underfunded schools in a high poverty community. I recall my amazing six-year-old students and the potential they brought to my classroom. I consider the parents' unwavering hope for their children's futures. I lament the opportunities they did not find in school, the stifling instruction that they reported, and the failed tests, low report card grades, and stringent behavioral policies that they recalled. This does not mean that they did not encounter wonderful and inspiring teachers. Every student in my sample described teachers that they loved and remembered with fondness.

As I worked with the children and their parents, I recognized that parents often interpreted children's schooling experiences differently than the children's teachers. Nespor (1997) identified a critical mismatch. Specifically, he highlighted what I believe is an important distinction between how parents and teachers make sense of children's school experiences. Nespor noted that "teachers' acquaintance with kids generally begins and ends within a single school year" and that the "histories of students in earlier grades are generally hidden from view" (p. 32). In contrast, he recognized that parents know children and live beside children across time.

In essence, parents witness children's long-term educational experiences as "kids matured and took their places in society" (pp. 31-32). Teachers know children for only short periods and often focus on children's academic skills and competencies. Each year, teachers face a new class of students that consumes their care and attention. Thus, parents' conceptions of time and schooling can collide with school conceptions of success and teachers' narrow conceptions of success can trump the embodied, multidimensional, and longitudinal knowledge of children brought by parents (Nespor, 1997).

My current role as a professor allows time for reflection that was rarely available to me as a classroom teacher. As a researcher, I regularly spend my mornings in a local coffee shop with my laptop computer and stacks of data – a luxury that was never part of my employment as a classroom teacher. Thus time – both in its passing and in terms of the amount of time available to reflect on the voices and experiences of children and their families – contributed how I now understanding children's school experiences.

INTRODUCING MARVIN

In preschool, Marvin and his older sister moved among his parents' home, foster care, and his grandparents' home. By the time Marvin arrived in my first-grade class, he had been retained once and had been living with his grandmother and his step-grandfather, Mr. Sherwood, who participated consistently in interviews across the ten-year project. Marvin's grandmother occasionally participated, interjecting comments and insights as she felt necessary.

The school served a low-socioeconomic community in the Northeastern United States. In the 1960's this community had been the site of race riots. Since then, the largely White immigrant population moved to the suburbs and housing projects were built for the remaining African American and Puerto Rican families.

Rosa Parks Elementary School served over 1200 children from the lowest socioeconomic community of what was then the eleventh poorest city in the United States; 97% of the children who attended my school qualified for free and reduced lunch. While this description may seem bleak, the community was also the home of thousands of families who worked diligently to feed, clothe, and educate their children.

Marvin's journey through school was often punctuated by altercations with other students and run-ins with teachers. While generally well-intended, he had a short temper and was often frustrated by academic demands. One summer during middle school, Marvin attended a summer reading camp that I hosted at a local college. He worked with a teacher candidate who had extensive experience working with adolescents who found school challenging. That summer he conducted a detailed investigation of banana slugs.

By high school, Marvin was increasingly attracted to vocational classes, especially those that involved woodwork. By the end of our time together, Marvin had been incarcerated for stealing a car and later for taking metal from a construction site. Apparently, he had moved out of his grandparents' apartment and moved in with mother who was struggling with addiction issues.

TEMPORAL DIMENSIONS OF THREE THEORIES

In order to explore the complex nature of being within time, I present three highly influential theoretical constructs that have informed our understandings and interpretations of actors in educational contexts; each references a dimension of time: timescales (Lemke, 2000), chronotope (Bakhtin, 1981, 1986), and habitus (Bourdieu, 1980/1990, 1991; Bourdieu & Passeron, 1977).

While I present the three theories separately, I recognize and will later examine the ways in which the experiences of time captured by these three theories overlap and intertwine for Marvin. Specifically, I explore the temporal affordances of each theory and highlight its potential to inform current understandings of how students craft possible selves and make sense of their worlds, including school.

LEMKE'S TIMESCALES

To explain long-term fundamental processes, including literacy development and schooling, Lemke (2000) proposed an ecological model that locates people within multiple, continuous, and simultaneous timescales ranging from the quick-moving microscopic changes to macro shifts of the universe.

To Lemke, these timescales are dimensions of an ecological system in which the lower levels are constituent of the higher levels with the higher levels involving conceptualizations and interpretations of lower level processes. Human semiosis, meaning making based on experience, involves interpretations of meanings that have been constructed and revisited over time.

Long-term processes, such as literacy learning and school affiliation, involve "fundamental changes in attitude or habits of reasoning"

(Lemke, 2000, p. 282) that cannot occur within short timescales. Lemke's notion of timescales challenges conventional models that conceptualize time as linear and cumulative, by arguing that people experience time in recursive and non-linear ways as they draw on lived events and various texts across multiple timescales to make sense of their worlds. Individual voices are fashioned out of available social resources from across time as people appropriate various discourses to serve their own purposes. As Lemke noted, "the language others speak to us, from childhood, shapes the attitudes and beliefs that ground how we use all our powers of action" (Lemke, 1995, p. 1).

In accordance with Lemke's theory, I argue that students draw upon multiple timescales to make sense of themselves and school. Specifically, Marvin draws upon familial timescales that reference the experiences of family members and his own past, alongside ongoing timescales that capture his lived experiences. Marvin and the people around him draw recursively and selectively on these multiple timescales. It is within this temporally charged context that Marvin understands the world and his role within that world. In the following analysis, Marvin drew upon discourses voiced over time to make sense of his experiences and to solve the challenges that he faced as a recently incarcerated youth.

THE LIBRARY AS AN ICON OF POSSIBILITY

When I spoke with Marvin at age 18, he had been released from incarceration four months earlier and was attending a vocational high school. Coming from an eighteen-year-old former high school dropout, his comments about the library were intriguing. Marvin explained, "Sometimes I might go to the library, me and a couple of my home buddies and a couple of my home girls." He continued, "Like the other day, we all went downtown because we had this big essay... and I looked up [information] on the computer" (Grade 10).

While a researcher conducting a short term study might interpret Marvin's enthusiasm for the library as a simple example of his renewed dedication to getting his life back on track, data from this longitudinal study locates the library as an icon of possibility extending back four generations. The accounts presented below draw upon multiple timescales and include memories of family members, accounts from Marvin's past, Marvin's ongoing experiences, and accounts that reference the future. Across Marvin's experiences, literacy, computers, the Internet, employment, and the future are all associated with the library.

At one of our early interviews when Marvin was in first grade, his grandfather, Mr. Sherwood, told a story that I originally interpreted as merely an account of the challenges he had faced in learning to read. Learning to read in elementary school had been difficult for Mr. Sherwood and his teachers were doing little to help. He later explained, "I was just mumbling through the whole thing [when I read in class] . . . that's when I told my mother about it. . . She said 'It's time for you to get a library card.' Every Saturday morning. . . we [Mr. Sherwood and his twin brother] had to go to the library and we stayed at the library until we picked up on our reading" (Grade 1).

Over the course of the ten-year project, the library was often referenced as a motif of possibilities:

> Mr. Sherwood: "We go to the library now. . . as a matter of fact, he spelt his name on the Internet." (Grade 1)

> Mr. Sherwood: I had to take her [Marvin's sister] to the library and he [Marvin] mentioned [that] his mind [was] really focused on the computers. . . Cause we was playing around on the [computers]. I just started learning on them about four years ago. I know how to do it. I went to the library and learned myself. (Grade 1)

> Mr. Sherwood: I used to take him to the library all the time. All the time, they love the library. It's a great place. . . . He's learned a lot about the Internet. (Grade 5)

Mr. Sherwood: Me and [Marvin's Grandmother] been trying to get him started going to the library you know. He [be] on [his] own [in] the neighborhood and stuff like that they [other family members] don't want him to go. But I want him [to] be responsible for himself so he can go and go to the library and get something and come on back. (Grade 8)

Mr. Sherwood: You got to start writing [on the computer] and start picking out what's this and that. (Grade 8)

Mr. Sherwood: I used to take him to the library, you know, get on the computers and stuff like that, but he got one upstairs now. (Grade 10)

While these comments recognize the library as a resource for literacy learning, they were also marked by words suggesting engagement and agency (e.g., "really focused," "they love the library," "getting involved," "responsible for himself"). For Mr. Sherwood, the library was a site of literacy possibilities.

The library not only helped Mr. Sherwood learn to read and offered similar opportunities to Marvin and his sister, it also provided Marvin and Mr. Sherwood with access to computers and thus possibilities for Marvin's future:

Mr. Sherwood: A computer is awesome. It's right now. It's the space age. You can't get around it. You just got to look in the paper, they want a computer programmer all that you know. (Grade 1)

Mr. Sherwood: He's trying, he's learned a lot about the Internet. . . .but I want him to get involved with [it] mainly like learn it [the computer]. (Grade 5)

Mr. Sherwood described the computers as "awesome," "right now," and "space age." He highlighted the importance of learning about computers by repeating the phrase "got to" and emphasized the connection between employment and learning to use computers.

Thus, the library carried meanings – related to literacy, computers, the Internet, employment, and the future – that were uniquely intertwined with and drew upon experiences at multiple timescales. Mr. Sherwood drew on his past when he recounted his own childhood experiences at the library and his hopes for Marvin's future. For a young man with a record of incarceration, visiting the library with friends was an agential act grounded in the past while simultaneously evoking future possibilities related to reading, books, computers, high school graduation, employment, and new friends who shared these interests and dreams.

While timescale analysis reveals how meanings are grounded in past experiences of family members, personal pasts, ongoing experiences, and perceived futures, this is only one dimension of a lived experience of time (Schatzi, 2006). Time is also experienced against the backdrop of institutions, the enacted mores of society, and the historical contexts that privilege particular ways of being and acting, as well as the embodied ways of being that people assume as a result of positionings and expectations.

BAKHTIN'S CHRONOTOPE

Marvin also operated within institutions, including schools that imposed temporal expectations. Bakhtin (1981, 1986) drew from philosophy, literary analysis, and linguistics, to explain how meanings are understood within complex social fields involving dialogic negotiations and unequal power dynamics. Bakhtin applied the construct of *chronotope,* which literally means *timespace,* to refer to "the intrinsic connectedness of temporal and spatial relationships" (Bakhtin, 1981, p. 84). Bakhtin explained that when authors create worlds they are obliged to draw upon the organizing categories of the real world – specifically recognizable time/space relationships.

Bakhtin identified and described literary genres based on how characters operated in time and space. He argued that these genres, or chronotopes, were constituted by the chronotopic motifs, or narrative tropes, that authors use and readers understand. These tropes might involve characters traveling along roads or paths as they move through narratives, unexpected encounters that change the directions of the stories, and nature as a symbol of pastoral and simpler worlds. These chronotopic motifs are meaningful because of the past literate and life experiences that readers bring to novels. As Bakhtin explained, conceptualizing possible meanings from stories requires passing thorough the "gates of the chronotope" (Bakhtin, 1981, p. 258) and drawing on pre-existing meanings to make sense of new experiences.

Motifs in Literacy and Schooling	Associated Meanings
Not reading fluently	Not proficient in reading, assumed to have difficulty com-prehending text, unsuccessful reader; poor public display of reading
Reading grade level texts	Proficient in reading, on-track, normal, successful, not in need of intervention
Failing standards-based English Language Arts examination	Being left behind, below standard, inadequate progress, literacy problem
Taking honors English course	Advanced, college track, capable, literate
Meeting criteria on standardized writing rubric	Proficient writer, college-bound, literate

Promotion/Retention	Success/failure, ability, normalcy, abilities correspond to age
Graduation	Accomplishment, success, achievement, grade attainment
Meeting grade level standards	Abilities commensurate with grade level, proficiency, successful
Special education	Failure in regular programs, needs extra help and additional time, slower pace, diminished potential
Vocational education	Salvageable, potentially worthy, academically challenged

Figure 1. A Sampling of Chronotopic Motifs in Literacy and Schooling

Chronotopic motifs also operate in schools, carry meaning, and have real life significance (see Figure 1). Promotion and retention carry meanings related to students' abilities. Being in third grade is embedded with the temporal expectations for being eight-years-old. Compensatory education and special education services suggest that some students require more time to learn (Heshusius, 1989; Hocutt, 1996).

In recent years, grade level standards, standardized testing at particular grade levels, and being able to read texts at particular levels have increasingly defined students relative to temporal expectations. Essentially, failure in school is not merely about what students can and cannot do; it is about what skills and strategies they display or do not display at particular points in time.

Just as chronotopes in literature shape the meanings of stories, chronotopes in school shape the meanings people construct about their lives and the lives of others. Failing to meet chronotopic expectations has real meanings and consequences for students in terms of their options such as honors classes, special education placement, or summer school, as well as their futures for college, employment, and income. Students are aware of the meanings associated with chronotopes of schooling and these meanings sediment, contributing to the ways in which students construct themselves and others as successful or unsuccessful.

However, chronotopes do not carry static and universal meanings. As Brown and Renshaw (2006) maintained, chronotopes continuously draw upon multiple available discourses and meanings and are experienced as hybrid syntheses that carry multiple meanings. Burton (1996) agreed; he presented chronotopes as interwoven, replacing one another, contradicting each other, and existing in complex interrelationships. Official chronotopes may suggest a particular reading of experience, however, other possible meanings grounded in marginalized perspectives exist in direct contention with dominant chronotopic readings (Burton, 1996).

In other words, while chronotopes of schooling, for example failing the fourth grade, have implicit meanings related to inability or immaturity that are generally recognized by school officials, chronotopes are always open to multiple interpretations and alternative readings – for example, failing fourth grade might be attributed to an incompetent teacher.

While Bakhtin's theoretical constructs of carnival and dialogism have been applied extensively to education (Ball & Freedman, 2004; Lensmire, 2000; Morris, 1994), the construct of chronotope has been used less frequently (for exceptions see Bloome et al., 2009; Brown & Renshaw, 2006; Mutnick, 2006). In the following section, I examine the construct of chronotope as a means to highlight time as context in schools. Marvin's failure to meet the expected chronotopes of schooling carried meanings that affected his school trajectory.

THE CONSTRUCTION OF FAILURE

When Marvin was five-years-old, he moved back and forth between his parents' and his grandparents' homes. Mr. Sherwood described this as a "negative experience... [Marvin] was going back and forth he didn't know where he was going" (Grade 1). Over the course of that year, he missed a lot of school and ended up repeating grade 1. Thus, when I met Marvin he was already a year behind in school.

Unlike most of the first graders, Marvin was already able to read when he entered my class. By June, he was well-prepared for second grade; however, Marvin again fell behind with reading. He failed both the 4th grade and the 8th grade State English Language Arts test. When in eighth grade, he read at the fifth grade level.

When Marvin was in fifth grade, he was identified as a behavior problem. Marvin was caught bringing a spray bottle of bleach to school. Marvin explained, "I brought the bleach to school to protect myself because he [another student] said he was going to get his brother and his other brother to jump me" (Grade 5). Marvin was suspended for several weeks. Later that same year, Marvin described a fight in which he broke a classmate's nose. Also in fifth grade, Marvin was diagnosed with ADHD and was placed on medication. While unconvinced that the medication would help, Marvin's grandmother was hopeful, "Cause he's a slow learner and he got this medication and that'll make him focus better" (Grade 5).

By eighth grade, Marvin was distraught and blamed his grandmother for allowing him to be placed in a special education class. Marvin noted that in special education classes the expectations were low, the pace of instruction was slow, and less work was assigned. His grandmother came to share Marvin's concerns. However, when she asked to have him placed back in the regular program, she was told that "he [would] have to work himself out" (Grade 8).

Ms. Sherwood viewed this situation as highly problematic and offered her own critique of the school's policy, "I've been reading up on it and they mostly put Black kids in them kind of classes and then they sunk them. And that's how you all [gesturing at Marvin who is sitting nearby] get behind" (Grade 8). While special education was presented as an opportunity for Marvin to catch up, Ms. Sherwood blamed special education for leaving Marvin behind.

When I returned to visit Marvin during high school, he had moved out of his grandparents' apartment and was living with his mother. Since I had visited him in eighth grade, he was arrested for stealing a car; later that year he was incarcerated for removing scrap metal from abandoned buildings. While I visited Marvin while he was incarcerated, data collection was suspended in accordance with IRB procedures until Marvin was released. Thus our final interview was held when Marvin was released and living with his grandparents. He was eighteen-years-old and entering the tenth grade.

However, despite this problematic school trajectory that resulted in Marvin being eighteen and faced with three more years of high school, Marvin and his grandfather rejected the official meanings that temporal disruption imposed on

Marvin. While failing to meet the official chronotopic motifs associated with school success, these messages of failure were complicated by the discourses of goodness and possibility repeatedly voiced by Mr. Sherwood:

> He on the ball... I mean he's sharp. (Grade 1)
>
> He is a sweet boy... He wants to help people out. (Grade 5)
>
> He's a very gullible person... Marvin ain't no bad person. (Grade 8)
>
> There was so many good things he had going in here [motions to his heart]. (Grade 10)

Mr. Sherwood spoke to chronotopic meanings imposed by school that characterized Marvin as incapable, unintelligent, and bad. He described Marvin as "on the ball," "sharp," "sweet," wanting to "help people," not a "bad person," and having "good things" in his heart.

While the verbs Mr. Sherwood uses are inconsistent in terms of their fortitude (e.g., "I hope" versus "I know") and various contingencies are recognized (e.g., sending him back to his parents, "if we can get to him"), Mr. Sherwood's sense of agency is strong, and given the right circumstances he is confident in his abilities to help

Marvin. Mr. Sherwood consistently extended this sense of agency to Marvin, noting his capacity to affect his own future:

> Mr. Sherwood: My main thing is "Marvin keep trying. Marvin, you do the best you can." (Grade 1)

> Mr. Sherwood: It's up to him... He's got to make that move... If he feel like he gonna do it... I *know* he can do it! (Grade 8)

> Mr. Sherwood: He had to make a difference hisself. And that's the secret. (Grade 10)

Bakhtin's construct of chronotope explains how people draw upon meanings that are embedded in meaningful motifs over time. Being retained in school, failing high stakes tests, falling behind with reading, being placed into special education, and incarceration are all temporal disruptions that defined Marvin as unsuccessful and resulted in his being three years behind at age 18.

While these disruptions were interpreted in particular ways and eventually coalesced to define Marvin's educational trajectory, Mr. and Ms. Sherwood challenged these meanings. They recognized alternative possibilities and potential. Not only were alternative accounts reiterated over time, but Mr. Sherwood also appealed to me, a researcher who had known Marvin for over ten years, saying "*you* know Marvin." While chronotopes carry meanings, those meanings are neither singular nor universal; they are open to interpretation and reflect people's beliefs and experiences.

Together timescales (Lemke, 2000) and chronotopes (Bakhtin, 1981, 1986) contribute to how we might understand the timescapes that accompany school. While timescale analysis (Lemke, 2000) highlights how meanings are constructed with and through the past, the present, and perceived possible futures and chronotopes, Bakhtin (1981, 1986) highlights the expectations that accompany those experiences, neither construct explains how ways of being are internalized and embodied over time which suggests yet another critical dimension of time.

BOURDIEU'S HABITUS

Throughout his life, Bourdieu (1971, 1980/1990, 1986, 1991; Bourdieu & Passeron, 1977) attempted to explain complex interactions between culture, social structures, and individual agency. His work focused on how social systems of domination persist and recreate themselves across time (Swartz, 1997). Bourdieu identified the construct of "habitus":

A system of lasting transposable dispositions which, integrating past experiences, functions at every moment as a *matrix of perceptions, apperceptions, and actions* and makes possible the achievement of infinitely diversified tasks. (italics in the original; Bourdieu, 1971, p. 83).

Habitus references how people's pasts are embodied in ways of being and knowing that accompany experience. Contrary to some interpretations of Bourdieu's work, people are not trapped in simple processes of social and economic reproduction (Albright, 2009).

Habitus is linked to the accumulation of cultural capital – ways of talking, acting, interacting and believing that privilege people in particular contexts. People who are able to accumulate large amounts of capital prior to seeking their place in the social/economic system have an advantage. Accumulation "depends on the length of time for which the family can provide him [the child] with free time, i.e., time free from economic necessity" (Bourdieu, 1986, p. 246). In addition, cultural capital is dependent "on the usable time (particularly in the form of mother's free time) available to it (by virtue of its economic capital, which enables it to purchase the time of others) to ensure the transmission of this capital" (Bourdieu, 1986, p. 253, parentheses in the original).

Bourdieu highlighted labor, patterns of consumption, and parent-child relations as conditions that inform habitus and in turn become the basis for the "perception and appreciation of all subsequent experiences" (Bourdieu, 1980/1990, p. 54). The factors that most significantly affect the development of habitus are subtle, involving non-verbal and unconscious ways of being, acting, and interacting including ways of looking, physical positioning, silences, and movements that are acquired unknowingly in the course of everyday activity (Bourdieu, 1991). While people can adapt their habitus to accommodate new situations, these changes are incorporated slowly and unconsciously as elaborations rather than drastic changes to existing dispositions (Bourdieu & Passeron, 1977).

While habitus is grounded in the past and involves limits and norms, it also acts "as an acquired system of generative schemes, the *habitus* makes possible the free production of all the thoughts, perceptions and actions inherent in the particular condition of its production" (Bourdieu, 1980/1990, p. 55). Habitus does not determine ways of being, acting, knowing, or believing, rather it evolves out of experiences and contributes to options made available within historical, social, and physical contexts. Habitus explains how individuals become whom they are – not through simple processes of reproduction – but through long-term participation in social structures and institutions that provide both affordances and limits for agency and identity.

Swartz drew on the work of Bourdieu to remind scholars that "not all social worlds are equally available to everyone" (Swartz, 1997, p. 107) and it is through habitus that prior life experiences teach people what may or may not be possible; agency is intertwined with past experiences. While researchers have readily applied Bourdieu's constructs of reproduction and capital to educational contexts (Dimitriadis & Kamberelis, 2006; Compton-Lilly, 2007; Lareau, 1989; Carrington & Luke, 1997), the construct of habitus, perhaps due to its longitudinal nature, has been less influential and rarely examined in-depth.

POSSIBILITIES OF BEING AND BECOMING

Habitus (Bourdieu, 1971) denotes the embodiment of dispositions across time; in the following account, we witness Marvin not only stating his desire to become a police officer, but also embodying ways of being that are consonant with this aspiration. For Marvin, being a police officer was grounded in a commitment to fighting injustice, interest in helping people, fascination with the job and the uniform, and his relationship with his grandfather. However, these dispositions were eventually challenged as Marvin negotiated multiple life experiences including interactions with police officers while incarcerated. Marvin's interest in becoming a police officer was reiterated across the study:

Mr. Sherwood: He want to be a policeman. (Grade 1)

Marvin: [To be a policeman, I need to] Go up in college and stuff [and read] the back of number cars [license plates] and when they have got crashed [and] the people get hurt and they [the police] try to figure out their names and stuff. (Grade 1)

Mr. Sherwood: I can speak for Marvin because I know what he want to do. . . He wants to help people. . . he always says he wants to be a police officer. He keeps on saying that all the time and stuff. I mean especially to help people. (Grade 5)

Mr. Sherwood: He wanted to protect and serve. (Grade 10)

Marvin's commitment to police work was not only consistently reflected in the words Mr. Sherwood used to describe Marvin's interest (e.g., "always," "keeps on saying") but it was also reflected in Marvin's actions. When Marvin was in first grade, Mr. Sherwood described Marvin's interest in watching "police stories" on TV:

He always [watches]. . . the highway patrol . . . He always talk about patrolmen. 'Cause I used to be a security guy he used to see me in my uniform and stuff like that so. . .

his personality that's what he's gonna be. (Grade 1)

Marvin's developing habitus reflected a commitment to police work that was grounded in his interest in helping and protecting people, and serving his community. When Marvin was young, his grandfather reported that Marvin wanted to "arrest his daddy and mother because they was doing bad things" (Grade 10).

When Marvin returned to school following the bleach incident in fifth grade, the school principal tried to encourage Marvin by making him the school's "public safety" – a role that resonated with his interest in police work. Each morning Marvin opened the parking lot gate for the teachers when they arrived in the morning.

Marvin's interest in being a police officer was also grounded in his sense of injustice. In first grade, he listed things at school that bothered him, "fighting, big bullies, taking pencils away from people, pushing people in line, hit-slapping people in the back of the heads" (Grade 1). In middle school, Marvin described the "bad kids" at his school:

They be cursing me. They be running around in the halls, fighting in the bathroom. And try to, pushing each other to get at the lockers. And with rubber bands they try to [Marvin snapped an invisible rubber band in my direction]. (Grade 8)

However, after being released from incarceration, Marvin was no longer sure that he wanted to be a policeman. Marvin explained, "I seen too many of them policemen." Despite his reservations about the police, he reported that law enforcement was "[still] kind of on my mind." At the time, he was applying for a job as a security guard, "If I get that security job, Grandpa, I'm telling you it's a wrap... I be having a flashlight. Yeahhhhh, yeah. I have a badge" (Grade 10). Ten years after Mr. Sherwood described Marvin as a six-year-old admiring his security guard uniform, Marvin ventriloquates those words referencing a badge and flashlight.

Following Marvin's incarceration, Mr. Sherwood was less confident about the possibility of police work. Mr. Sherwood reported, "He ain't got no plan now" (Grade 10). Marvin raised several possibilities including being a lawyer, nurse, or a carpenter.

Concerns about Marvin actually becoming a police officer first appeared when Marvin was in grade 8. This was the year Marvin was placed in special education; he continued to experience discipline problems at school. At the same time, Mr. Sherwood often commented on Marvin's ability to work with his hands:

Mr. Sherwood: He's good with it [his hands] . . . he know how to fix a lot of bicycles. (Grade 8)

Mr. Sherwood: Vocational school I think would be best for him you know like an engineer or something like that. Cause he like to tear-up things and try to put them back together again. (Grade 8)

Mr. Sherwood: He liked to work on cars. . . he would tear stuff up, demolition, he loved it. (Grade 10)

Mr. Sherwood: He told me this morning, we was talking said he loves it [his vocational education classes]. (Grade 10)

While beginning in grade eight Mr. Sherwood highlighted Marvin's vocational abilities, Marvin was not convinced. While Marvin enjoyed his vocational education classes and was proud of his abilities, he struggled to retain his dreams of becoming a police officer. Simple and logical decisions, like becoming a carpenter, are not all that simple. They are caught up with the embodied selves constructed over long periods of time and contextualized within people's experiences.

Bourdieu (1986) maintained that a person's habitus is deeply rooted into a person's past and changed slowly over long periods of time. As evident in the accounts presented above, helping people and being a police officer reflected strong dispositions that were deeply rooted in Marvin's beliefs about himself and the world. While Marvin retained his dreams of becoming a police officer, these dreams were complicated by his arrest record.

Neither complete nor comprehensive, together timescales (Lemke, 2000), chronotope (Bakhtin, 1981, 1986), and habitus (Bourdieu, 1971, 1980/1990, 1986, 1991) illustrate the multiple dimensions of time. Time is not a simple linear sequence. It is not a just resource that can be invested and translated into learning. It is not simply a gauge against which student learning can be measured. As Adam (1989) explains, time's significance is multidimensional:

> Time enters into every tiniest aspect of that moment. It is implicit in waiting, in planning, in contemplating, and in guilt; just as it is central to memories, the language structure, and to the speech as it was happening. (p. 468).

As Marvin's experiences illustrate, it involves ways of making sense of the world, the expectations that accompany our experiences, and ways of being that contribute to who we are and who we become.

WHAT DO THEORETICAL UNDERSTANDINGS ABOUT TIME OFFER EDUCATORS?

While I maintain that the multidimensional nature of time has not been fully explored by educational researchers, educational researchers have not ignored time. Some have treated time as a methodological variable. For example, Roberts, Jurgens, and Burchinal (2005) examined the extent to which home literacy practices of young children predicted later language and literacy skills. In their study, which followed children from age 18 months through their entry into kindergarten, they treated time as a methodological variable – the length of the intervention. In an earlier study, conducted by Leseman and de Jong (1998), children were tracked from ages four to age seven to examine the relationship between home literacy practices and educational outcomes. Assessments were administered repeatedly at planned intervals of time to ascertain the stability of established home literacy practices.

Other researchers have focused on development across time. Classic studies in developmental psychology (e.g., Kohlberg, 1981; Piaget, 1953) identified stages that children progress through and/or benchmarks that children were expected to meet at particular points in time. Developmental perspectives focus on change over time and the degree to which individual change reflects expected pattern of development. Thus time has historically been treated as a methodological variable that could be controlled and should be considered rather than as context in which people operate.

Still other researchers have acknowledged the significance of history, and recognized time within people's life stories. Critical race theorists (Dixson & Rousseau, 2006; Ladson-Billings & Tate, 1995) critique ahistorical accounts of schooling and arguing that current educational practices are deeply rooted in policies, practices, and attitudes of the past. Ladson-Billings (1994) situated her research with successful teachers of African American children within discussions about the historical segregation of African American and White students. She maintained that successful teachers challenged accepted beliefs, narratives, and instructional practices creating new possibilities for students.

Life story researchers, including McAdams (2001), argue that people's identities are conceived and expressed as stories that involve reconstructions of people's pasts alongside ongoing experiences and anticipated futures. Life stories are continuously constructed and reconstructed within social and cultural contexts. People's life stories are to a strong degree retrospective; individuals tell these stories to themselves and others to make sense of their worlds and themselves.

While life story researchers recognize the social nature of storytelling and the cultural contexts in which people live, they do not document how people exist and operate within time, the ways identities are constructed and reconstructed across time, or the ways time contextualizes people's lives.

In addition, time has been recognized as a consideration in discussions of educational practice. Time has historically been conceptualized as a resource that can be invested to increase learning. In the late 1800's, William T. Harris, then the U.S. Commissioner of Education, lamented the shortened length of school days and years (NECTL, 1994); he argued that that students would learn more if they spent more time in school.

Between 1910 and 1930 the efficiency movement attempted to make American businesses and schools more productive – producing more in less time (Callahan, 1962). Efficiency initiatives included the adoption of standardized achievement tests to monitor students' progress, rating systems for teachers, and policies that would ensure that time was not wasted, for example by minimizing transition time between classes and limiting the time students spent at the blackboard. These initiatives became the basis for contemporary schools that featured class periods and lecture-style classrooms.

Responding to arguments that unproblematically associate more time with increased learning, Slattery critiques what he calls the "exaggerated emphasis on manipulation of time" (Slattery, 1995, p. 612):

> time management, timed tests, wait time, time on task, quantifiable results over time, time schedules, time-out discipline centers, allocation of instructional days on annual school calendars, core academic time, Carnegie units, time between classes, year-round schooling, and the like. (Slattery, 1995, p. 612-613)

Time is not merely a resource that can be divided up, allocated, and manipulated. Time is not like money; it cannot be invested, accumulated, or saved (Adam, 2003b). Slattery proposed a vision of time as:

> ... radically eclectic, determined in the context of internal relatedness, recursive in its complexity, autobiographically intuitive, aesthetically intersubjective, phenomenological, experiential, simultaneously quantum and cosmic, ironic in its kaleidoscopic sensibilities, and ultimately, a hermeneutic search for greater understanding that motivates and satisfies us on the journey. (p. 631)

Time encompasses everything that people have lived and understood as well as the ways they make sense of themselves, their experiences, and their relationships. Slattery (1995) argued that educators must focus on "allowing the process of becoming, rather than the artificial demands of clocks and linear sequences, to dominate our personal and professional lives" (p. 616).

Neither researchers nor practitioners have attended to how people draw upon events at multiple timescales to make sense of their worlds, to negotiate the temporal expectations of schooling, or reference deep-seated dispositions that inform students' ways of being.

Above, I have presented three theoretical frameworks that explore various dimensions of time as context. Timescale analysis calls attention to events and the construction of meaning across multiple timescales as Marvin makes sense of himself and his experiences. This analysis revealed visiting the library as a recurring motif that was loaded with meanings grounded not only in Marvin's experiences, but also in experiences and stories that could be traced back to his step-great-grandmother.

These experiences related not only to literacy, but also to technology and possibilities for the future. Looking back across time and forward towards Marvin's future reveals negotiations among family members, peers, and school expectations that come together as Marvin chooses to visit the library. His actions are neither random nor arbitrary; they are selected from a range of possibilities offered by a particular present and a lived and interpreted past in the service of a possible future.

Chronotopic motifs related to literacy and schooling draw attention to how official definitions of school success reference time. Marvin's teachers interpreted temporal disjunctures as an indication that Marvin was slow, learning disabled, and a vocational student. Despite these positionings being repeatedly challenged by Marvin and his grandparents, over time, official disjunctures accumulated and limited Marvin's future educational options.

As Adam (2003a) argued, "embodied time is lived and experienced alongside, despite of, and in conflict with the culturally constituted social relations of time" (p. 61). The temporal expectations for children, grounded in rhetorics of standards, benchmarks, and No Child Left Behind (2001) are assumed to be universal – temporal expectations are not negotiable. While official meanings associated with chronotopes of schooling had real effects on Marvin's life, Marvin and his grandparents challenged these meanings and offered alternative readings of situations and events.

Finally, Bourdieu's construct of habitus highlights the process of becoming and the ways early experiences and beliefs are deeply engrained, embodied, and slow to change. Despite experiences in school and with the legal system that could be interpreted as evidence that police work was not a good fit, Marvin did not abandon his interests and the draw of the badge, helping people, and addressing injustice continued to inform his goal of becoming a security guard.

Challenging accounts that present children's future goals as arbitrary, habitus draws attention to the process of becoming as well as how goals and possibilities are deeply infused with self. Bourdieu's theories situate habitus within inequitable social fields (e.g., urban schools, high poverty communities) that privileged forms of capital that Marvin did not possess. Marvin's lack of economic capital (money), social capital (influential social networks), and institutional capital (a high school diploma) complicated the challenges he faced in realizing his goals.

While each of these theories highlights a particular dimension of time, together they provide an initial framework for understanding of how time operates in people's lives: timescales as layered experiences that people draw upon to make sense of their worlds; chronotopes as involving official temporal expectations; and habitus as embodied ways of being. These frameworks invite researchers to recognize the various manifestations of time and to recognize the role time plays in long-term processes such as literacy learning, identity construction, school trajectories, school achievement, and occupational aspirations.

Longitudinal qualitative research and temporal analyses offer important insights that explain the effects of long-term situations such as living in high poverty communities and attending poorly funded schools. Attention to time allows us to view students as eternally changing and growing. By attending to time, we recognize that the disillusioned teenager was once an enthusiastic first grade student. Rather than knowing a student at a certain time and place, attending to time allows us to view children across time in multiple situations and settings.

Finally, Marvin's story demonstrates the permanence of hope. While teachers and researchers may be inclined to dismiss particular children as incorrigible or uneducable, Marvin and his grandfather retained faith in his future. Despite repeated setbacks, temporal disruptures, and institutional policies that complicated Marvin's trajectory and limited his options, Marvin and his grandfather retained hope for the future, for example by visiting the library, taking vocational education classes, and returning to high school.

These enactments of hope and agency are grounded in the faith Marvin's grandparents had in Marvin and the faith Marvin retained in himself. Marvin is much more than an eighteen-year-old, African American, low income youth – he is the six-year-old who wanted to be a police officer, the little boy who loved storybooks, the child who brought bleach to school to protect himself from bullies, the middle school student who was fascinated by banana slugs, the special education student who was not challenged, and the talented vocational education student who was "good with his hands."

Attending to time allows us to view children as complex, nuanced and multifaceted people with rich histories and experiences. For Marvin, time as context reveals agency, lost opportunities, challenges, strengths, resilience, and hope.

While I present Marvin's experiences in relation to each of the three dimensions of time, these dimensions overlap and intersect. If we revisit Marvin and his dream to become a police offer, we witness an embedded habitus that supports this disposition. However, we also witness a school system filled with expectations and tracked instructional experiences that have been described as a school to prison pipeline (Wald & Losen, 2003; Winn, 2011).

Thus expectations related to school contributed to how Marvin came to define himself. The instructional experiences he experienced – heavy-handed discipline, low expectations, special education placement, retention, and racism – informed his sense of self and the dispositions that he brought forward. In addition, Marvin drew on past timescales (e.g., watching police shows with his grandfather, seeing his grandfather in his security uniform), and future possibilities suggested by the public library, as he made sense of himself – a recently incarcerated youth. Thus, the three dimensions of time identified in my analysis are intricately intertwined and reciprocally informative.

In order to recognize how students, educators, and researchers exist within time, we must move beyond simple equations that associate more time with increased learning. If we accept the premise that people make sense of their lives within and across time, we begin to acknowledge the importance of not just the here and now, but of considering children's longitudinal experiences in school in terms of educational policies, practices, and research. We recognize communities and families as bringing rich histories, sets of experiences, and understandings that are grounded in long term relationships with schools and literacy. We begin to understand that these experiences and the meanings that surround them exist within chains of events, experiences within institutions, and embodied ways of being.

What might a research agenda involve that recognizes time as critical to making sense of children's school experiences and literacy learning? Such an agenda has implications for theory, methodology, and educational practice. Theoretically, literacy researchers must:

1. Work to recognize and explain further manifestations of time in literacy learning;

2. Move toward a comprehensive understanding about the ways time operates in the lives of children, teachers, and in the evolution of schools, literacy instruction, and the field of education; and

3. Bring together scholars from various fields that share an interest in time including developmental studies, new literacy studies, sociology, historical educational studies, sociohistorical theory, and critical race theory to explore issues related to literacy learning.

Methodologically, we must:

1. Produce more longitudinal research, allowing more researchers opportunities to examine how time manifests itself in the experiences of students, educators, families, and in communities;

2. Develop and refine methodologies that access past and future experiences to understand how participants make sense of the present;

3. Explore methodologies that consider change and consistency, trajectories and disjunctures, setbacks and growth; and

4. Interrogate issues related to funding, tenure, and scholarship that work against researchers conducting long-term studies and thus attending to time.

Significantly, expanded notions of time invite educators and scholars to think about inequity "because time is largely taken for granted and therefore invisible, the social relations of time can continue to maintain existing inequalities and create new one in the globally constituted world" (Adam, 2003b, p. 119). As Lemke maintained, "We construct meaning of our lives ... across multiple timescales of action and activity, from the blink of an eye to the work of a lifetime" (Lemke, 2005, 110). Our challenge as researchers and educators is to recognize and attend to temporal complexity to support teachers and their students across time and as they move through school.

Appreciation is extended to the Spencer Foundation for their support of the final phase of this research project

REFERENCES

Adam, B. (1989). Feminist social theory needs time. Reflections on the relation between feminist thought, social theory and time as an important parameter in social analysis. *The Sociological Review, 37*(3), 458-473.

Adam, B. (2000). The temporal gaze: the challenge for social theory in the context of GM food. *The British Journal of Sociology, 51*(1), 125-142.

Adam, B. (2003a). Reflexive modernization temporalized. *Theory, Culture, and Society, 20*(2), pp. 59-78.

Adam, B. (2003b). When time is money: Contested rationalities of time in the theory and practice of work. *Theoria: A Journal of Social and Political Theory*, 94-125.

Albright, J. (2009). Problematics and generative possibilities. In J. Albright & A. Luke (Eds.), *Pierre Bourdieu and Literacy Education.* Mahwah, NJ: Lawrence Erlbaum.

Bakhtin, M.M. (1981). *Four essays by M. M. Bakhtin* .C. Emerson C. & M. Holquist (Trans.).

Austin, Texas: University of Texas Press.

Bakhtin, M.M. (1986). *Speech genres and other late essays.* M. Holquist & C. Emerson (Eds.). Austin, Texas: University of Texas Press.

Ball, A. & Freedman, S.W. (Eds.). (2004). Bakhtinian perspectives on language, literacy, and learning. Cambridge, UK: Cambridge University Press.

Bidart, C. (2012). What does time imply? The contribution of longitudinal methods to the analysis of the life course. *Time and Society, 22*(2), 254-273.

Bloome, D., Beierle, M., Grigorenko, M. & Goldman, S. (2009). Learning over time: Uses of intercontextuality, collective memories, and classroom chronotopes in the construction of learning opportunities in a ninth-grade language arts classroom. *Language and Education, 23(4),* 313-334.

Bourdieu, P, (1971). Systems of education and systems of thought. In Young MFD (Ed.) *Knowledge and control* (pp. 189-207). Berkshire, UK: Open University Press.

Bourdieu, P. (1980/1990). *The logic of practice* (R. Nice trans). Stanford, CA: Stanford University Press.

Bourdieu, P. (1986). The forms of capital. In Richardson J.G. (ed.) *Handbook of theory and research for the sociology of education* (pp. 241-258). New York, NY: Greenwood Press.

Bourdieu, P. (1991). *Language and symbolic*

power (G. Raymond & M. Adamson trans.). Cambridge, MA: Harvard University Press.

Bourdieu, P. & Passeron, J. (1977). *Reproduction in education, society, and culture.* London: Sage.

Brown, R. & Renshaw, P. (2006). Positioning students as actors and authors: A chronotopic analysis of collaborative learning activities. *Mind, Culture and Activity 13(3)*: 247-259.

Burton, S. (1996). Bakhtin, temporality, and modern narrative: Writing "the whole triumphant murderous unstoppable chute." *Comparative Literature 48(1):* 39-64.

Callahan, R.E. (1962). *Education and the cult of efficiency.* Chicago, IL: University of Chicago Press.

Carrington, V. & Luke, A. (1997). Literacy and Bourdieu's sociological theory: A reframing. *Language and Education, 11(2),* 96-112.

Cipriani, R. (2013). The many faces of social time: A sociological approach. *Time and Society, 22*(1), 5-30.

Compton-Lilly, C. (2003). *Reading Families: The Literate Lives of Urban Children.* New York, NY: Teachers College Press.

Compton-Lilly, C. (2007). *Re-Reading Families: The Literate Lives of Urban Children, Four Years Later.* New York, NY: Teachers College Press.

Compton-Lilly, C. (2012). *Reading Time: The literate lives of urban secondary students and their families.* New York, NY: Teachers College

Press.

Compton-Lilly, C. (2016). *Reading students' lives: Literacy learning across time*. New York, NY: Routledge.

Dimitriadis, G. & Kamberelis, G. (2006). Pierre Bourdieu. In G. Dimitriadis & G. Kamberelis (Eds.), *Theory for Education*, (pp. 65-73). New York: Rutledge.

Dixson, A.D. & Rousseau, C.K. (2006). *Critical race theory in education: All God's children got a song*. New York: Rutledge.

Ekwall, E. E., & Shanker, J. L. (1993). *Ekwall/Shanker reading inventory* (3rd ed.). Boston, MA: Allyn & Bacon.

Facer, K., Joiner, R., Stanton, D., Reid, J., Hull, R., & Kirk, D. (2004). Savannah: mobile gaming and learning? *Journal of Computer Assisted Learning, 20*(6), 399-409.

Firth, R. & Robinson, A. (2014). For the past yet to come: Utopian conceptions of time and becoming. *Time and Society, 23*(3), 380-401.

Giddens, A. (1991). *Modernity and self-identity*. Cambridge, MA: Polity Press.

Heshusius, L. (1989). The Newtonian mechanistic paradigm, special education, and contours of alternatives: An overview. *Journal of Learning Disabilities, 7*, 403-415.

Hocutt, A.M. (1996). Effectiveness of special education: Is placement the critical factor? *The Future of Children, 6*(1), 77-102.

Keightley, E. (2013). From immediacy to intermediacy: The mediation of lived time. *Time and Society, 22*(1), 55-75.

Kohlberg, L. (1981). *Essays on Moral Development, Vol. I: The Philosophy of Moral Development.* San Francisco, CA: Harper & Row.

Ladson-Billings, G. (1994). *The dreamkeepers: Successful teachers of African American children.* San Francisco, CA: Jossey-Bass Publishers.

Ladson-Billings, G. & Tate, W.F. (1995). Toward a critical race theory of education. *Teachers College Record, 97(1),* 47-68.

Lareau, A. (1989). *Home advantage: Social class and parental intervention in elementary education.* London: Falmer.

Lemke, J. (1995). *Textual politics: Discourse and social dynamics.* New York, NY: Taylor and Francis.

Lemke, J. (2000). Across the scales of time: Artifacts, activities, and meanings in ecosocial systems. *Mind, Culture, and Activity, 7(4),* 273-290.

Lemke, J. (2005). Place, pace and meaning: Multimedia chronotopes. In Norris S. & Jones R. (Eds.), *Discourse in action: Introducing mediated discourse analysis* (pp. 110 – 122). New York, NY: Routledge.

Lensmire, T. (2000). *Powerful writing, responsible teaching.* New York: Teachers College Press.

Leseman, P. & DeJong (1998). Home literacy: Opportunity, instruction, cooperation, and socio-emotional quality predicting early reading achievement. *Reading Research Quarterly, 33(3),* 294-321.

Leslie, L., & Caldwell, J. (2006). *Qualitative reading inventory - 4.* Boston, MA: Pearson.

McAdams, D.P. (2001). The psychology of life stories. *Review of General Psychology, 5(2),* 100-122.

Morris, P. (1994). *The Bakhtin reader: Selected writings of Bakhtin, Medvedev, Voloshinov.* London: Arnold.

Mutnick, D. (2006). Time and space in composition studies: "Through the gates of the chronotope." *Rhetoric Review, 25(1),* 41-57.

National Education Commission on Time and Learning [NECTL]. (1994/2005) Prisoners of time. Washington, DC: ED366115 [Available on-line at: http://www.ed.gov/pubs/PrisonersOfTime/index.html]

Nespor, J. (1997). Tangled up in school: Politics, space, bodies, and signs in the educational process. London: Routledge.

No Child Left Behind Act [NCLB] (2001). Washington, DC: Retrieved July 8, 2009, http://www.ed.gov/nclb/landing.jhtml

Piaget, J. (1953). *The Origins of Intelligence in Children.* London: Rutledge & Kegan Paul.

Roberts, J., Jurgens, & Burchinal (2005). The

role of home literacy practices in preschool children's language and emergent literacy skills. *Journal of Speech, Language and Hearing Research,* 48(2), 345-359.

Schatzki, T.R. (2006). The time of activity. *Continental Philosophy Review, 39,* pp. 155-182.

Slattery, P. (1995). A postmodern vision of time and learning: A response to the National Education Commission Report, Prisoners of Time. *Harvard Educational Review,* 65(4): 612-633.

Strauss, A. & Corbin, J. (1990). *The basics of qualitative research: Grounded theory procedures and techniques.* Newbury Park, CA: Sage Publications.

Swartz, D. (1997). *Culture and power: The sociology of Pierre Bourdieu.* Chicago, Illinois: Chicago University Press.

Wald, J., & Losen, D. J. (2003). Defining and redirecting a school-to-prison pipeline. *New directions for youth development, 2003*(99), 9-15.

Winn, M. T. (2011). *Girl time: Literacy, justice, and the school-to-prison pipeline. Teaching for Social Justice.* New York, NY: Teachers College Press.

AN INTERVIEW WITH CATHERINE COMPTON-LILLY
BOBBIE KABUTO

BOBBIE
Why did you become interested in studying time and literacy?

CATHERINE
In my original research, which became my doctoral dissertation, I was focused on 10 kids in my first-grade classroom. At first, I just wanted to document their home and school literacy practices. My theory was – and this was based on several years of teaching in the school – that even though they were from a very poor community they had very strong families. The families really did care about the kids, so I wanted to document the literacy practices in their homes. After I defended my dissertation, I became curious about

the kids and went back to find them four years later, and then three years later, and then three years later.

So I ended up having this longitudinal data set. The more I considered the data set, the more I started thinking about what it means to "become" over time. How do people construct not only identities but also how do they interact with the world? What does the world mean to be a particular person in a particular space? I started asking these sorts of questions.

In sociocultural theories, we think a lot about context. When I think about scholarship in which people have discussed context, they often present context as either physical or social spaces. Context is often treated as the present in which things happen. I really try to complicate this idea of context by attending to time and how we make sense of the world as we operate across time.

For example, you are not just listening to me right now, and making sense of what I'm saying based on the words that are coming out my mouth. In your mind, you may be remembering something you read last week, or something that happened to you when you were six-years-old. You may be thinking ahead to what you're going to be doing later. So our minds are putting things together within longitudinal temporal contexts.

This idea of context has significance, particularly for children who have been historically underserved because they're living within a legacy that has created particular structures in schools and in society. So, I think about these children as being located within inequitable histories. In short, inequity doesn't happen in first grade or high school; inequity has been and continues to be constructed over time. There is a longitudinal trajectory in which some kids get access to resources and others don't.

BOBBIE
How does this work fit into the larger scope of family literacy, which has been the crux of your work?

CATHERINE
If you go back and look at what I consider the two quintessential volumes on family literacy, both of them have very strong longitudinal dimensions. In particular, I'm thinking of Denny Taylor's early work in her book *Family Literacy*. In that book, she spends a whole chapter on parents talking about their past experiences learning to read, and how those experiences inform what they do with their children. You get a generational form of prolepsis – a relationship between the parents' past and the child's present, alongside the parent's hopes for the child's future. So there is a rich temporal dimension of family literacy.

The other person whose work resonates with family literacy is Shirley Brice Heath. Her book,

Ways with Words, was longitudinal, in that she worked in the communities described in her book for over seven years. In recent years, Shirley Brice Heath published a newer volume where she describes going back to find the families from *Ways with Words*, and revisits the families 40 years later. Thus, family literacy has temporal dimensions that we must recognize and honor.

Another slippery term for all of us to define and get our heads around is culture. We like to reduce culture to things, like food or festivals. I argue that the concepts of culture and family are similar in many ways. For example, there are powerful longitudinal dimensions of culture. What you bring forward and what gets passed on to the next generation is the "stuff" that transcends our particular time and space. Culture is always changing and it constantly hybridizes with other spaces and people.

BOBBIE

How do you differentiate between *longitudinal* and *ethnography* in the discussion of time? Within longitudinal research, researchers may say longitudinal is one year. Sometimes longitudinal is over three years, and sometimes longitudinal is a lifetime. Ethnographies look at social and cultural interactions within context over time.

CATHERINE

Good question, and I would throw in one additional term – revisiting.

I will try to talk through these terms. With ethnography, you immerse yourself in the community, cultural group, school, or classroom. You're living there and you are attempting to witness what it is like to be there. You might be studying what we call culture – the culture of the space, the classroom or community. You might be examining language or literacy practices in that space, but you're immersing yourself in that space. If you do that over a long period of time while attending attend to change over time, then I would say that your work is both ethnographic and longitudinal. However, you could occupy a particular space for years, but never attend to what is changing or emerging. Longitudinal research attends to time and change. Ethnography might not. That's how I distinguish between the two.

In contrast, I think the work that I did with the families from *Reading Families* is a revisiting study. I went back every three or five years. I didn't really follow the children. Instead, I captured snapshots every few years. I then tried to link the pieces of the puzzle together. For it to be longitudinal, I would have to follow those families and work with them much more often.

So I try not to use the term longitudinal to describe my own work. I argue that *Reading Families* and my other books related to these families are not truly longitudinal. In contrast, the newer study that we are doing with immigrant families is longitudinal. In that study we visit families two or three times each year.

BOBBIE
To go along with our discussion of time and change, how do you think the field of literacy has changed over time?

CATHERINE
Well, I've been working with Rebecca Rogers and Tisha Lewis Ellison on a meta-ethnography that asks that question. A few years ago, we conducted a review of family literacy research, which was published in the *Reading Research Quarterly*. In that review, we examined how diversity has been treated in family literacy scholarship. But that wasn't the piece we intended to write. We wanted to do a meta-ethnography. George Noblit and Dwight Hare created meta-ethnography as a methodology for looking across qualitative studies.

For quantitative meta-analysis, you often examine effect sizes. For meta-ethnography, you analyze the metaphors that people use to describe and present their research. What metaphors are used to explain findings? What metaphors are used to explain the data? What metaphors are used by participants? Here's an example: "funds of knowledge" is a metaphor. Funds of knowledge can be accumulated and you can invest it. It is an economic and financial metaphor, although we rarely consider its economic meanings.

Becky, Tisha, and I have identified the top-cited scholars in the field of family literacy. Basically, we identified seven researchers whose work is routinely cited by family literacy scholars. We then examine one seminal article written by each scholar to explore its metaphors. We then track those metaphors to see how they change over time, and we think we're finding some interesting insights into the field.

Basically, we determine whether a given metaphor is maintained, refuted, or extended over time. The earliest piece we analyzed was Denny Taylor's (1982) and the newest piece was Kate Pahl's (2002). For example, one metaphor that shows up in scholarship conveys the idea that literacy learning is natural. If you look at Taylor's work, she uses multiple naturalistic metaphors. If you track the use of naturalistic metaphors over time, what is considered natural and what it means to be natural changes. In the early work, literacy itself is natural and children learn literacy naturally. Whereas, when you look at Luis Moll's work, the teacher is identified as a natural mediator between home and school. If you examine Pahl's work, you continue to find natural metaphors but they reference the geological notion of sedimentation. In her work, we are invited to attend to growth alongside established structures that are more permanent and enduring.

So, yes, I believe that the field of family literacy is changing as we learn more and continue to consider the range and breath of literacy practices in families and communities.

LIST OF SELECTED WORKS BY CATHERINE COMPTON-LILLY

Compton-Lilly, C. (in press). Reflexive layers and longitudinal research: The Case of Christy. In M. Grenfell & K. Pahl (Eds.), *Language-Based Ethnographies and Bourdieu.*

Compton-Lilly, C. (in press). Revisiting development: Insights from a longitudinal research project. In A. Woods and B. Exley (Eds.), *Literacies in Early Childhood.* Australia & New Zealand: Oxford University Press.

Compton-Lilly, C., Kim, J., Quast, E., & Tran, S. (in press). Transnational literacy practices in immigrant families: A longitudinal study. *Journal of Early Childhood Literacy.*

Compton-Lilly, C., Papoi, K., Venegas, P., Hamman, L., & Schwabenbauer (2017). Intersectional identity negotiation: The case of young immigrant children, *Journal of Literacy Research, 49*(1), 115-140.

Compton-Lilly, C. (2017). Exploring literacy and identity at multiple timescales. In P. Albers (Ed.) *Global conversations in literacy research* (54-67). New York, NY: Routledge.

Compton-Lilly, C. (2017). *Reading students' lives: Literacy learning across time.* New York, NY: Routledge.

Compton-Lilly, C. (2016). The possibilities of longitudinal research: Lessons from a teacher and a researcher. *The Educational Forum, 80,* 466-478.

Compton-Lilly, C. (2016). A Closer Look at a Summer Reading Program: Listening to Students and Parents. *The Reading Teacher, 70*(1), 59-67.

Compton-Lilly, C. (2016). The development of literacy practices across a decade: Families, friends, and schools. In D. Appleman & K. Hinchman (Eds.), *Adolescent literacy: A handbook of practice-based research.* New York, NY: Guilford Publishing.

Compton-Lilly, C. (2015). Longitudinal studies and literacy studies. In J. Rowsell & K. Pahl (Eds.), *Routledge handbook of literacy studies* (pp. 218-230). New York, NY: Routledge.

Compton-Lilly, C. (2015). Reading lessons from Martin: A case study of one African American student. *Language Arts, 92*(6), p. 401-411.

Compton-Lilly, C. (2014). The development of writing habitus: A ten-year case study of a young writer. *Written Communication, 31,* 371-403.

Compton-Lilly, C. & Halverson, E. (Eds.). (2014). *Time and space in literacy research*. New York, NY: Routledge Publishers.

Compton-Lilly, C. & Gregory, E. (2013) Conversation currents: Family literacy. *Language Arts, 90*(6), 464-472.

Compton-Lilly, C. & E.B. Graue, with R. Rogers & T.Y Lewis. (2013). Agency, authority, and action in family literacy scholarship: An analysis of the epistemological assumptions operating in family literacy scholarship. In J. Larson & J. Marsh (Eds.), *Handbook of early childhood literacy, 2nd Ed.* London, UK: Sage Publications.

Compton-Lilly, C. (2013). The Temporal Expectations of Schooling and Literacy Learning Jermaine's Story. *Journal of Adolescent & Adult Literacy. 56*(5), 400-408.

Compton-Lilly, C. (2013). Temporality, trajectory, and early literacy learning. In K. Hall, T. Cremin, B. Comber and L. Moll (Eds.), *International handbook of research on children's literacy, learning and culture* (pp. 83-95). West Sussex, UK: Wiley-Blackwell.

Compton-Lilly, C. (2012). *Reading time: The literate lives of urban secondary students and their families*. New York, NY: Teachers College Press.

Compton-Lilly, C., Rogers, R. & Lewis, T. (2012) Analyzing epistemological considerations related to diversity: An integrative critical literature review of family literacy scholarship. *Reading Research Quarterly, 47*(1), 33-60.

Compton-Lilly, C. (2011). By the book and behind the glass: Teacher self-regulation in one reading intervention. *Language Arts, 88*(6). 429-438.

Compton-Lilly, C. (2011). Time and reading: Negotiations and affiliations of a reader, grades one through eight. *Research in the Teaching of English, 45*(3), 224-252.

Compton-Lilly, C. & Greene, S. (Eds.). (2011). *Bedtime stories and book reports: Connecting parent involvement and family literacy.* New York, NY: Teachers College Press.

Compton-Lilly, C. (ed.) (2009). *Breaking the silence: Recognizing the social and cultural resources students bring to the classroom.* Newark, Delaware: International Reading Association.

Compton-Lilly, C. (2007). *Re-Reading families: The literate lives of urban children, four years later.* New York, NY: Teachers College Press.

Compton-Lilly, C. (2004). *Confronting racism, poverty and power.* Portsmouth, NH: Heinemann Publishers.

Compton-Lilly, C. (2003). *Reading families: The literate lives of urban children.* New York, NY: Teachers College Press.

CATHERINE COMPTON-LILLY
A SHORT BIOGRAPH

Catherine Compton-Lilly is the John C. Hungerpiller Professor at the University of South Carolina. As a professor in the College of Education, Dr. Compton-Lilly's research has focused on family literacy practices, particularly the literacy practices of children from communities that have been underserved by schools.

In her initial work, she documented the home and school literacy practices of eight of her former first grade students as they moved from elementary school through high school. In a current study, now in its tenth year, she is exploring the family literacy practices of children from immigrant families.

She has edited or authored eight books and has authored multiple articles related to family literacy in major literacy journals including *the Reading Research Quarterly, Research in the Teaching of English, The Reading Teacher, Journal of Early Childhood Literacy, Written Communication, Journal of Literacy Research* and *Language Arts*.

Dr. Compton-Lilly has a passion for helping teachers to support children in learning to read and write. Her interests include early reading and writing, student diversity, and working with families. She has a strong interest in teacher education and is currently documenting the exceptional teacher education practices at the University of South Carolina. She holds emerita status at the University of Wisconsin Madison.

BOBBIE KABUTO
A SHORT BIOGRAPHY

Bobbie Kabuto, Ph.D. is Professor of Literacy Education and Department Chair of the Elementary and Early Childhood Education Department at Queens College, City University of New York. She was the 2019 recipient of the United Kingdom Literacy Association (UKLA)/Wiley Research in Literacy Education Award and the Senior Editor for the Garn Press Women Scholars Series.

Her research interests include the relationships among early bi/literacy, socially constructed identities, and language ideologies. She currently works with families of struggling beginning readers and writers.

Her work has been highlighted in journals such as *Reading Research Quarterly*, the *Journal of Early Childhood Literacy*, and *Early Childhood Research and Practice*. Her first book *Becoming Biliterate: Identity, Ideology, and Learning to Read and Write in Two Languages* was published by Taylor and Francis in July 2010.

GARN PRESS WOMEN SCHOLARS SERIES

NEGOTIATING A PERMEABLE CURRICULUM: ON LITERACY, DIVERSITY, AND THE INTERPLAY OF CHILDREN'S AND TEACHERS' WORLDS

Negotiating a Permeable Curriculum: On Literacy, Diversity, and the Interplay of Children's and Teacher's Worlds is part of the Garn Press Women Scholars Series. Originally printed in 1993 in the National Council of Teachers of English (NCTE) Concept Paper Series, *Negotiating a Permeable Curriculum* revisits Dyson's powerful concept of a permeable curriculum, a socially constructed learning space created by teachers and children.

Negotiating a Permeable Curriculum is a timeless piece as it is relevant to current moves in education with the implementation of the Common Core State Standards (CCSS). In 2010, the CCSS were released as a set of standards devised to create national benchmarks of student knowledge and skills in literacy and math. While not specifically mentioning curriculum, the CCSS explicitly outlines what should be taught from kindergarten to grade 12 and, therefore, it has had a major impact on establishing a national curriculum and assessment system led by private, corporate companies.

Challenging the standardization of learning, Dyson ask readers to push back the "curricular curtain" to wonder about the complex social and intellectual work in which children engage when they become writers. The emphasis on becoming focuses on how learning to write is always a dynamic state, as children learn about themselves while they learn about written language. In *Negotiating a Permeable Curriculum*, Dyson provides concrete examples of the social and cultural challenges learning to become writers entails. Dyson highlights how teachers can enact a permeable curriculum so that the worlds of teachers and children come together in instructionally powerful ways.

TEACHING WITHOUT TESTING: ASSESSING THE COMPLEXITY OF CHILDREN'S LITERACY LEARNING

Teaching without Testing: Assessing the Complexity of Children's Literacy Learning by Denny Taylor is the second book in Garn Press Women Scholars Series. This book revisits Taylor's seminal and influential work based on her Biographic Literacy Profiles Project. *Teaching without Testing: Assessing the Complexity of Children's Literacy Learning* is a timely book that challenges the scientific assumptions of standardized testing in developing effective instruction to meet the literate lives of all students.

Through detailed observations of student learning, Taylor encourages readers to consider alternative ways of assessing children's reading and writing based on observable literacy behaviors. Supporting a humanistic perspective to the education of children, Taylor argues that standardized and diagnostic methods of assessment and teaching, based on test-driven, cooperate-led accountability practices, have detrimental effects on children and result in the de-professionalization of teachers.

TIME IN EDUCATION: INTERTWINED DIMENSIONS AND THEORETICAL POSSIBILITIES

Time in Education: Intertwined Dimensions and Theoretical Possibilities is part of the Garn Press Women Scholars Series. It explores the intersection of literacy and the construct of time within education through the scholarship of Catherine Compton-Lilly, who highlights the complexity of studying learning. In particular, she focuses on how and what people learn over time within school-based structure, which entail established power structures that define who we are as learners, privileging some learners and marginalizing others.

Catherine Compton-Lilly presents a theoretical kaleidoscope of learning and literacy over time and illustrates how understandings of learners and learning shift as educators cast their gaze through different theoretical lenses. She asks how people reconcile, or strive to reconcile, complementary and contradictory framings of learners—a dilemma often faced by educators and parents.

Specifically, Compton-Lilly proposes that time acts as a constitutive dimension of people's experiences that significantly affects how people make sense of their worlds by exploring the temporal affordances of three highly influential theories: Jay Lemke, Mikhail Bakhtin, and Pierre Bourdieu. To illustrate the temporal potential of these theories, she draws upon data from a ten-year case study of one student and his family. Attending to how people operate within time provides important insights into longitudinal processes including identity construction, literacy learning, and becoming a student. These insights are important not only to researchers who attempt to make sense of the experiences of children and teachers, but also to educators who must seek ways to acknowledge and effect the longitudinal trajectories of children.

GREAT WOMEN SCHOLARS: YETTA GOODMAN, MAXINE GREENE, LOUISE ROSENBLATT, MARGARET MEEK SPENCER

Reading as a transactional process, reader-response, the ways texts teach, miscue analysis, kid watching, social responsibility and imagination, our existential existence, I am not yet, not yet, are all ideas that are part of who we are, but would not be without Yetta Goodman, Maxine Greene, Louise Rosenblatt, and Margaret Meek Spencer.

On Friday, September 21st 2001, ten days after 9-11, Yetta, Maxine, Louise, and Margaret spoke about their lives and work, what makes teaching sublime, and about the dark side of imagination. To keep hope alive, to continue to imagine life as it could be otherwise, and for the sake of future generations and ourselves, it is important that we read what they had to say and continue to learn from them.